PRAISE FOR JACQUELINE PIRTLE

"Jacqueline takes you always directly to what you are ready to see or experience."

— LONGTIME CLIENT AND READER

"It is liberating to face your own blocks and to be finally free of the weight that they have caused for many years. And while for me the changes I'm experiencing are noticeable and real, I still feel like myself. Just a more sure self."

— LONGTIME CLIENT AND READER

"Jacqueline makes me BELIEVE I can be and live a joyful and magical existence every new day of my life!"

— LONGTIME CLIENT AND READER

The *365 Days of Happiness* bestselling author

JACQUELINE PIRTLE

BRAGGING

Because you're worth it!

A 30 day journal

COPYRIGHT

Copyright © 2021 Jacqueline Pirtle
www.FreakyHealer.com

All rights reserved. No part of this book may be reproduced or transmitted in any form or by any means, electronic or mechanical, including photocopying, recording, or by any information storage and retrieval system without the written permission of the publisher, except where permitted by law.

ISBN-13: 978-1-955059-21-3

Publisher: Freaky Healer

Editor-in-chief: Zoe Pirtle
All-round Support: Mitch Pirtle

Book cover design by Kingwood Creations kingwoodcreations.com

Author photo courtesy of Lionel Madiou madious.com

I want to let you know that all my books and holistic practitioner work together, as a wholesome system, are supporting you to live a more conscious, mindful, and happier life.

However, I made it so you can receive the benefit of living more joyously solely by working through this terrific journal book, while also experiencing the full satisfaction in continuing on to the next journal of this series—not to mention the rock solid tools you get by reading any of my other books or adding in my podcast *The Daily Freak*. Either way, I know you'll love my inspirational teachings.

Find out more at:
FreakyHealer.com
Amazon - Jacqueline Pirtle's Author Page
The Daily Freak Podcast

Before you dive in, I want to thank you for hopping on the magic train with me! I truly hope you enjoy ***Bragging*** as much as I loved writing it, and if you do, it would be wonderful if you could take a short minute and leave a review on Amazon and Goodreads.com as soon as you can.

Your kind feedback helps other readers find my books more easily, and to be happy faster. Consider it a joy-deed for the world.

Thank you!

ACKNOWLEDGMENTS

Let's be honest here… I have a dream team!

I could not have finished this book without the help of talented, creative, high-for-life, and phenomenal professionals.

From the bottom of my heart, I want to thank Zoe Pirtle for her editorial mastery; Mitch Pirtle for his all-round support; kingwoodcreations.com for their fun and polished book cover design; and madiouART.com for an amazing photo shoot.

I'd also like to extend a huge "Thank You!" to all fans of my work and books—I created this beautiful journal series for you.

Life is spectacular with you on my side!

BE the self-bragger you are meant to be!

DEDICATION

I dedicate this journal to all those thinking that bragging is hard, or not OK, and challenge them to make bragging their lifestyle!

INTRODUCTION

Proud bragger,

It is high-time for this journal to exist—a bragging, gloating, gushing, and filling-your-pride-to-the-brim kind of workbook.

I'm over the moon happy to say, "Here it is!"

It is also long overdue to put a stop to all misunderstandings and negative meanings about the *art of aligned bragging* or being in love with oneself and life to the extent of behaving in a manner of feeling full of oneself.

How much better can it get than someone showing up as the best version of themselves and the most self-loving ever, when as a matter of fact, everything is *ONE* and the same energy, always connected and sharing at all times—meaning that they share and spread their boasting happy self with everything and everyone and are uplifting the whole world because of it?

I say nothing else is better than that—for them and for all!

Sure, misaligned bragging exists and that version of gloating never feels good, but what we are focusing on in this journal is the aligned boasting which feels incredible and is what everyone is here - in physicality - to choose, and also to enjoy.

INTRODUCTION

So how amazing is it that, by living through the naturally well-feeling bragging ways that you are about to create in this journal, you will spread your love for yourself and your life - and the fun that you are having - to everything and everyone, lifting the whole world into a higher state, or at least as high as your surroundings want to go with you?

I say that's pretty cool!

Bragging helps you to overcome your old habits of selling yourself short while inspiring you to dream big, then even bigger, and to feel your own personal power everywhere and at anytime —inviting you to go for the best of the best at all times.

There, an ocean of opportunities will catch hold of you, inviting you to dive deep. Just think of that incredible match-up and shift into the higher frequency of bliss, by being *ONE* with the excitement of living a fun life filled with incredible manifestations.

A bragging way of life gives your best version of you the spotlight—all while changing at a constant and vivid speed, in flow with how life naturally happens. I'm inspired to think that this is what you really want and who you truly are here to BE and live as.

Journaling through this 30 day ***Bragging*** workbook brings huge calibrations into the equation so you can experience life like you never have before, craft a time beyond your expectations, and love what you live—to the extent of becoming a master in living consciously and mindfully, feeling phenomenal while manifesting the best of the best.

It's a change that is forever!

As a side note, there are a couple of bonus days at the end in case you ever find the need to do two in a day, or so you can keep working while you wait for the next journal in this series to arrive. I also left you a few blank **bragging** pages to journal about deepening your ways of being proudly alive.

Enough chit-chat, I know you are ready—so grab your pen and have incredible fun with catching more life than you have ever caught, in your new crazy ways.

Happiest,
    Jacqueline

 ay 1

IMAGINE yourself behind closed doors - not locked - and even though you are in a comfy and cozy room, you have a sense of limitation, of being tucked away and not as free as you could be. You are grateful being in such a wonderful room, but deep inside you know that behind those doors is a way of being YOU that is so much more than you are now—more colorful, fun, inspired, and more alive. Simply *more*! If you only could just sneak a little peek, or even better, say "YES!" to going through those doors. Out of the blue you decide, "I'm going for it! I'm taking my chances!" How does this feel—now that you have made the decision to go for *more* in life, and *more* as you? Get your more-experience on paper and be ready, because tomorrow you will make the majestic leap into your new way of living your free and bragging life.

_____
_____
_____
_____
_____
_____
_____
_____
_____
_____
_____
_____

Bragging - Because you're worth it!

Day 2

FILLED to the brim with excitement of your thrilling decision to fly higher than you have ever before say, "I can't wait!" and grab those door handles with your willing hands. Start turning the knobs, while feeling that your true adventure awaits and knowing it will be one of a kind! Keep at it until the doors spring open—embracing you with an invitation to walk through. With a smile and a deep breath, and in a knowing trance, you start your essential walk jam-packed with the understanding that your inner being is guiding and pulling you towards your best life ever. Go on, this is your glorious tunnel of freedom in which you walk to liberate yourself, leaving all chains from your old ways behind. With every forward-step you take your gorgeous tunnel brightens and you feel lighter than ever. Prepare yourself for the brightest show to be at the end of your walk of liberty; the entrance into your new bragging life! How does your freedom feel? Journal, liberator, journal!

Get excited because tomorrow, your arrival in your new world of being *outside those doors* and showing up fully as you is the main attraction.

_____
_____
_____
_____
_____
_____
_____

Bragging - Because you're worth it!

# Day 3

PEEKABOO! Open your eyes and realize that today is the day where you made it—home! You took a chance, you walked the walk, now here you are. You have arrived in your perfect world for you—where you are your true you and will brag all the way to the millions of stars about yourself and your life, because after all, that is what you came here to do in this journal and in your life. You came to be so full of yourself and so sure about yourself that insecurities, criticism, or denials - yours or anybody else's - are jobless and can't exist. How does this feel, to be freely you? Are you exited to start bragging with pride? How much do you love, respect, accept, appreciate, and thank yourself in this new world—and will you go all out to do it more? Write, beautiful new bragger, write!

Tomorrow we'll get rid of the negative old beliefs attached to bragging—but today you need not worry at all. Instead, you'll brag for, and about, yourself without any limits.

_____
_____
_____
_____
_____
_____
_____
_____
_____
_____
_____

Bragging - Because you're worth it!

Day 4

Let's burry the downer meanings of bragging!

Think about the energy that the word *bragging* comes with—a feeling of security and sureness, knowing yourself, and being a big, huge, and humongous person; but it's also uplifting and fun-spilling. It shows respect, appreciation, acceptance, gratitude, and love for youself—while seeing a bigger life and purpose, and the ability and willingness to BE more and live more. What a powerful energy! Write about the beautiful meanings that bragging has for you - now that the old nonsense and negativity is straightened out - and list your newfound expectations for yourself and your life.

___
___
___
___
___
___
___
___
___
___
___
___
___
___
___
___

Bragging - Because you're worth it!

ay 5

BRAGGING REPRESENTS your pride for yourself and shows how much fun you are actually having in your life—even more potently, how much phenomenal-ness you are open to allow-in for yourself. Let's start with pride today—we will tackle *fun, being open, and allowing-in* over the next few days. Go deep into what being proud of yourself really means to you! Is it self-love, letting go of traumas and pains, and being freer than you have ever been? Journal, proud one, journal!

___
___
___
___
___
___
___
___
___
___
___
___
___
___
___
___
___
___

Bragging - Because you're worth it!

 ay 6

HOW MUCH FUN do you really have in life, and how much more of it do you want? What could bragging about yourself have to do with getting bliss into your life more often? Would gushing about your gorgeous heart - how big it is - and your grand love it holds be of fun-value? Or could bragging about your talent of being a flamenco dancer - while in truth you can't dance to save your life - be a fun thing to enjoy? How will you create an unlimited amount of joy, giggles, and laughter in your new world?

___

Bragging - Because you're worth it!

# Day 7

YOU HAVE TO BE AN OPEN-MINDED, open-hearted, open-worded, and open-hearing, open-feeling, open-tasting, open-smelling, and open-to-everything-in-life kind of person in order to be a bragger who loves to brag—not to mention being on the light side of life to not take everything so seriously. Why? Because all else puts roadblocks in your way by giving you excuses not to gloat about yourself and your life. So, how open can you be - or become - to really, really fly high as your own personal bragger?

___
___
___
___
___
___
___
___
___
___
___
___
___
___
___
___

Bragging - Because you're worth it!

 ay 8

ALLOWING yourself to stand on the highest pedestal - or at least five stacked high - and feel amazing for yourself is the master golden key to living a great life, besides being the portal to let wonderfulness in. So allow yourself to brag about your amazingness! But wowzers there is so much more; shouting out to the whole world that you are incredible - not that the world *needs* to know since all that matters is your unshakable inner knowing - brightens the globe with your undeniable shiner abilities and incredible essence of light. Are you that allowing? How much higher will you allow yourself to go, and what more do you want for yourself?

_____
_____
_____
_____
_____
_____
_____
_____
_____
_____
_____
_____
_____
_____
_____

Bragging - Because you're worth it!

Day 9

LET'S talk about the action of bragging since most would love to brag a little - or a lot - more and it's time to come out of the shame-room and see the art of bragging about yourself and your life in a new and truthful light. When you brag, you love yourself, you are standing in and up for yourself, and you are designing and also creating good - actually the best - for yourself—aside from aligning with the true worth that you really are. How will you practice your biggest and boldest bragging action yet?

_____
_____
_____
_____
_____
_____
_____
_____
_____
_____
_____
_____
_____
_____
_____
_____
_____

Bragging - Because you're worth it!

 ay 10

BRAGGING IS VERY personal and is asking for a laser sharp focus on yourself, and only on yourself! Looking left or right at the world, or others, can get you back into your cozy room behind those doors—because not everyone has discovered the fun of bragging yet, and the old stigma of *being over the top is bad* still exists in physicality. The best way to get the hang of gloating is to make it a private matter at first. So without saying anything to anyone, start bragging to yourself about yourself and your life—once rooted in this fun way of living, you can take it with sureness further into the world. What are you going to brag about first, and then after?

Bragging - Because you're worth it!

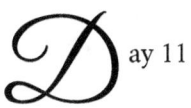 ay 11

BEING a professional bragger means that you are blessing others and the whole world into a higher frequency because you shift to BE and live in a heightened way when you gloat—given that your bragging comes from your pure heart. Everything is energy - the same energy - and constantly connected, sharing and spreading their energy. See, you uplift everything and everyone by loving yourself so much that you have to say something. I say, keep bragging even more!

Bragging - Because you're worth it!

 ay 12

Why do others get upset when you brag? By showing the world how much you love yourself and your life you highlight how little others love themselves and enjoy their lives. You shine a light onto how much more everyone could BE and live, and how much more fun life could be, digging up their shortcomings of living and blowing old beliefs into nothing-ness. You are outshining them! It's like one bulb being brighter than the other —but even if the brighter bulb would be dimmed, it would not make the other lighter. Never dim your bragging. Instead, keep giving them hints to brag too since only they can shine their light brighter. Your bragging is a brightening gift to the world—how will you manage that?

_____
_____
_____
_____
_____
_____
_____
_____
_____
_____
_____
_____
_____
_____
_____

Bragging - Because you're worth it!

 ay 13

BRAGGING IS DONE BEST when you are aligned with your inner being - with who you really are - and fully in the sense of what is best for you and feels fitting, so that the bragging is believable. If your gloating is impure, or your bragging is about being better than others, it will be of an un-well feeling nature—which is not the way to go. How can you stay on top of making this about you, and only you?

___

Bragging - Because you're worth it!

# Day 14

FEELING your bragging and what you are bragging about is a must in order to get the whole benefit of this wonderful way of living. Brag, but then also stop to breathe and feel how upwards shifted you sense yourself by gloating without remorse. Remember, it is an art to brag; treat it as a conscious and mindful practice of being you. How will you do that?

Bragging - Because you're worth it!

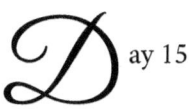 ay 15

SEEING YOUR BRAGGING, the bragging that is always present, and everything that is there to brag about is a visionary gift that you must claim—and that your eyes want to give you the enjoyment of. So use those peepers and see bold and high! What do you see?

___

Bragging - Because you're worth it!

 ay 16

THINKING ABOUT YOUR BRAGGING CONSCIOUSLY, while giggling about the *more* of you that is showing up to the world, is worth the experiment of bragging the biggest and boldest ever. Be prepared for the awe of what such a gushing can achieve, the life it will create, and the wellness you are invited to indulge in. Go experiment, bragger, then journal about your wisdom!

Bragging - Because you're worth it!

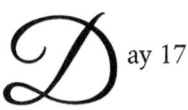 ay 17

SMELLING and tasting what bragging represents for you will let you enter a culinary phenomenal-ness—since these two senses are important to live your life. So why not go out of your old ways and into what bragging foods and drinks are for you? List please! Then devour them with a bragging "mmm" and "ahh," while noticing with amusement how the world reacts to your enjoying.

Bragging - Because you're worth it!

 ay 18

HEAR YOURSELF BRAG, and notice the up-lifted and huge energy you become when you are in your gushing action. Listen to the birds and all of nature, giving you a free crash course in how to gloat—just think of the impressive little bee. Be aware of the bragging motorcycle and such—inspiring you to go big too. Catch what's there, incredible bragger!

Bragging - Because you're worth it!

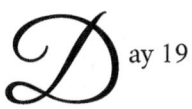 ay 19

"TODAY IS THE BEST DAY EVER!" Now *that* is some high-for-life bragging right there—meaning that today, you will brag the best way ever. So what will you say? What will you gloat about? Can you go even better? Today, tomorrow, and then every day after? Brag big, journaler!

Bragging - Because you're worth it!

Day 20

WHENEVER YOU FEEL LOW, all you have to do is brag and immediately you will feel high and higher. It's an all-by-yourself-superpower! Initiating your bragging while alone in front of a mirror works well—start bragging, look at your bragging self, and give it a nice applause. Or rip open your front door and go out into the world—to brag and then brag some more about yourself, your life, and all that is there to brag about. Bragging about other people, your kids, partner, and family is a regal and uplifting action too—but best done only after you have fulfilled your own self-bragging job. What's your favorite way here?

Bragging - Because you're worth it!

 Day 21

BRAGGERS ARE CHOOSERS! Choosers are powerful! Powerful is in your nature! When you brag you choose to feel amazing and that is sheer mighty-ness because it means you understand that you are fully responsible for how you feel and how you live your life —and that no matter what, you can always shift to experience everything in a better way. What are you choosing to brag about? And how do you feel being so high up?

___

Bragging - Because you're worth it!

Day 22

"WHAT'S TO BRAG ABOUT?" you might ask. Well, there is your breath, heart, organs, or skin that are worth a gloat. There is your physics - even if it's your pinky toe - that are excellent bragging partners. Plus, there's your inner being that is always bragging about you, so why not brag back a little? Gush about your clothes and all the material physical life things—they are not to be forgotten. How about nature, surprising you every day with different weather, animals, conditions, colors, and learning—very worth boasting about, especially when telling a story of wading through strong wind, hail, or rain to get home safely. That's being a true champion! Then there are others that love to be bragged about—you get that high essence too, since everyone always shares their energies with everything. Bragging is a powerful and uplifting practice—best thing is, you can always choose to boast at all times.

Bragging - Because you're worth it!

 ay 23

FUN FACT IS, that in every new split second everything is always new—and that includes you, too! It's the normal way of how life works, meaning that you can always brag anew and anew. So no matter if you just bragged about something a second ago, a new second just arrived and your new bragging can take shape. Have some fun here and unless it gets on your nerves, what's the big deal of re-bragging, especially when what you are gloating about is of such glorious nature?

_____
_____
_____
_____
_____
_____
_____
_____
_____
_____
_____
_____
_____
_____
_____
_____
_____

Bragging - Because you're worth it!

 ay 24

How would a bragging song sound to you? What words would it include? No need to be a singer or songwriter, just go for it and produce your "I'm a bragger!" song—then belt it, baby! Don't forget to invite your loved ones.

___

Bragging - Because you're worth it!

 ay 25

WHEN YOU MEET ANOTHER BRAGGER, what is your first reaction? Is it annoyance—about their bragging or their sureness about themselves? Are you filled with pain and sadness in your own heart because you are back in your comfy room behind closed doors? Are you inspired and fired up by their energy—filling yourself and bragging higher too, since there is never anything wrong with latching onto such a heightening energy? What is your response? Become aware, while never forgetting that your reaction will naturally always be different. Your awareness is what we are hinting at here!

Bragging - Because you're worth it!

 ay 26

COME up with an elevator pitch of how to brag about yourself and your life in 3 minutes—your catching brag life story that tells who you are and the boasting force you bring to the table. Create a different one for work, home, being a parent or partner, and one for everyday or special days. Use your finest bragging styles here!

_____
_____
_____
_____
_____
_____
_____
_____
_____
_____
_____
_____
_____
_____
_____
_____
_____
_____
_____
_____
_____

Bragging - Because you're worth it!

Day 27

WHEN WAS the last time you bragged about your physical body and your health? No matter the state you are in right now, you have to start somewhere. Best is to find the most boastable part, then start saying things like, " I have the strongest body ever," or "I am the smartest person I know," or "my lungs breathe the most powerful air in and out." Do this privately until you are rooted as such—then, take it public and even further and don't forget to shout it into the universe with delight. You will be amazed at how your physical well-being can change with speed by utilizing such a gloating practice—makes sense because, after all, you are filling every single cell of your whole being with powerful energy. It can't get any better than that—list your parts please!

Bragging - Because you're worth it!

Day 28

HAVE you ever noticed a teeny tiny bird singing from the top of its lungs—soundly, loudly, and not to be missed? That is boasting at its best, staring you in the face. It really couldn't get any clearer. Do the same! Be that bird—not to be overlooked or under-heard. How will you do that?

_____
_____
_____
_____
_____
_____
_____
_____
_____
_____
_____
_____
_____
_____
_____
_____
_____
_____
_____
_____
_____

Bragging - Because you're worth it!

# Day 29

PAIN IS WORTH BRAGGING ABOUT, but only to yourself since most individuals do not gloat about the gold that can come from pain! It goes something like this; "Wow, my back pain is of immense power and wisdom, such strong force of nature showing me what's so heavy on me lately," or; "My headache asks the world of me in such a fantastic way—to take ruthlessly better care of myself," and; "My vertigo shows me strongly how dizzy I am with my alignment. I better take this thriving sign and listen to it." You see, every symptom is the language of your physical body to communicate what exactly it is that you need to do for yourself. Worth a bragging moment, don't you think?

___

Bragging - Because you're worth it!

 ay 30

As I sit here writing this book, I see you as your huge mountainous bragging you—as a sure, bold, knowing, aligned, happy, successful, healthy, and abundant being. What a sight! Now, if I can see you that way, you surely can find a way to see yourself that way too and latch onto this wonderful truth of yours!

How does that feel? What do you see in yourself? How powerful are you, and what are you going to do, now that you have realized your worth and value?

Also, what are your deepest wishes and desires? Make your glorious list! Then come up with bragging ways, words, actions, thoughts, and feelings that support what you fancy so much.

Are you bragging about yourself yet? Go over-gloating here—after all, you want to shift into your high-for-life frequency!

_____
_____
_____
_____
_____
_____
_____
_____

Bragging - Because you're worth it!

* * *

Ready to continue on your self-growth path? Get the next journal in this series: ***Of Course! Because why wait...***

BONUS

Because hey, nobody ever wants the goodness to end.

Keep on bragging—it really suits you!

ay 31

THROUGH YOUR BRAGGER HEART AND coming from your truth-saying lips, repeat after me, "I am me and they are they—and I stay me even when they are they!" Can you be alert enough to stays focused on yourself, and only on yourself—no exceptions? Why? Because too much peeking left or right is not good for your bragging self. How will you stay focused on you?

___

Bragging - Because you're worth it!

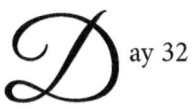ay 32

YOU ARE A LIMITLESS BRAGGER! At least as your energetic you, living in your physical body and experiencing physicality—your inner being always has more to brag about. Knowing that, are you putting a cap onto your bragger abilities because you live with the old belief of being limited? I say, cut it out!

Bragging - Because you're worth it!

 Day 33

CAN BRAGGERS ALSO BE NAY-SAYERS, negative-ers, and down-ers? Yes they can—but it's bragging into an un-well direction and you don't want to be part of it. Instead, jump ship! Then steer away - alone if you must - to get to shore where aligned bragging that fits your style is happening. The disaligned? Let them be.

Bragging - Because you're worth it!

 ay 34

As the bragger that you are, do you take enough time to get better at your gloating-craft? Because just like everything else, it takes time to become the best of the best—while also feeling and believing in yourself that you are the strongest ever. How are you going to make time for gushing?

Bragging - Because you're worth it!

 ay 35

THINK about the gloating power of the universe inviting you, as a bragger yourself, to co-create and have the most thrilling fun while at it! Things can't get any more exciting than that! Go on, how does that feel? What are you going to do - or stop doing - while being in such a strong partnership?

___

Bragging - Because you're worth it!

AND NOW IT'S YOUR TURN!

The following are your magical pages to become your own unstoppable bragger-boss!

I'm counting on you to go full-of-yourself here!

 ay 36

BRAGGING IS COOL BECAUSE...

Bragging - Because you're worth it!

 Day 37

BRAGGING FEELS GOOD BECAUSE...

___

Bragging - Because you're worth it!

ay 38

BRAGGING MAKES ME HAPPY BECAUSE…

___

Bragging - Because you're worth it!

 Day 39

BRAGGING IS HEALTHY BECAUSE...

Bragging - Because you're worth it!

ay 40

BRAGGING IS the best ever because…

___

Bragging - Because you're worth it!

* * *

Don't forget to leave a review on Amazon.com and Goodreads.com as soon as you can, as your kind feedback helps other readers find my books easier. Thank you!

ALSO BY JACQUELINE PIRTLE

365 Days of Happiness

Because happiness is a piece of cake!

This passage book invites you to create a daily habit to live your every day joy, and is the parent companion to *365 Days of Happiness*, the journal workbook.

* * *

365 Days of Happiness - Special Edition

Because happiness is a piece of cake

This beautiful Special Edition of the bestseller *365 Days of Happiness: Because happiness is a piece of cake* has room for your notes after every daily passage.

* * *

365 Days of Happiness - Journal Workbook

Because happiness is a piece of cake

This enlightening journal workbook is your daily tool to create a habit of living your every day bliss, and is the companion to *365 Days of Happiness: Because happiness is a piece of cake*.

* * *

Life IS Beautiful - Here's to New Beginnings

If you like digging deeper into the meaning of life and are inspired by spirituality, then you'll love Jacqueline's effective teachings.

* * *

Parenting Through the Eyes of Lollipops
A Guide to Conscious Parenting

If you like harmony at home and laughter in the house, then you'll love Jacqueline's inspirational methods.

* * *

What it Means to BE a Woman
And Yes! Women do Poop!

If you like to live free, empowered, and want to decide for yourself, then you'll love Jacqueline's liberating ways.

* * *

Life-changing Journals

What. If. - Turning your IFs into it IS!
Open - Where it all starts!
To BE and Live - The reason you are here!
High for Life - The best case scenario!
Of course - Because why wait!

Every journal comes in two lengths:

A 30 day journal

A 90 day journal - The Extended Edition

If you like being in charge of your own life, turning your dreams into reality, enjoy journaling, and want to squeeze the most out of your time, then you'll love Jacqueline's uplifting teachings.

ABOUT THE AUTHOR

Bestselling author, podcaster, and holistic practitioner, Jacqueline Pirtle, has twenty-four years of experience helping thousands of clients discover their own happiness. Jacqueline is the owner of *FreakyHealer* and has shared her solid teachings through her podcast **The Daily Freak**, sessions, workshops, presentations, and books with clients all over the world. She holds international degrees in holistic health and natural living. Her effective healing work has been featured in print and online magazines, podcasts, radio shows, on TV, and in the documentary *The Overly Emotional Child by Learning Success*, available on Amazon Prime.

For any questions you might have, to sign up for Jacqueline's newsletter, and for more information on whatever else she is up to, visit www.freakyhealer.com and her social media accounts @freakyhealer.

www.ingramcontent.com/pod-product-compliance
Lightning Source LLC
Chambersburg PA
CBHW071423070526
44578CB00003B/670